Swimming This

Christine Swint

FUTURECYCLE PRESS

www.futurecycle.org

Published by FutureCycle Press
Lexington, Kentucky, USA

ISBN 978-1-938853-65-4

For Sean, Casey, and Dylan

Contents

IV. Suburban Llorona

V. The Red Weaver

I. Forbidden Egg

Forbidden Egg, Found and Thrown Away

Shifting from the new tightness of her jeans,
    a girl squats near a creek, gathers pebbles, tosses them.
The water weaves dark tapestries among the rocks.

She imagines heaven as a real place,
    like a French baroque painting, she would say
if she knew the words, where angels, men, and women

dance the minuet in leather pumps. With kid gloves on
    they touch, then bow to each other. They smell like sunshine.
With a fingernail she pries a gold stone out of clay,

thinks about angels in powdered wigs
    and robin's egg blue frock coats. She weighs
the stone in her palm, wedges a thumbnail

into a crack in the clay-stained amber surface to see
    if it will split, and it does—an egg, an ancient locket.
The darkness inside the gold locket never ends.

As if through a spyglass, she stares into the dark
    for signs of life—she conjures a woman who sheds
a red gown and lies near a stream, legs open in a V.

The red gown scares the girl. A man crouches over the naked
    woman. His arms are muscled, streaked with dirt.
She skips the egg across the creek, and it sinks into the swirls.

My Parents' Courtship, 1958

He walked to her house on a night
so dark, he couldn't have seen his hand
until he approached the cone of light
at the corner, the asphalt a slick sea
turning ever blacker beyond the pocket
of electric bulbs eying the empty street.

Entering the shadows of the street,
he'd have ducked his head in a trench of night,
from his house to hers a private pocket
of time, of solitude, when her hand-
some running back didn't have to see
his own jawline in the mirror. Lamplight

from the bay window spilled a diamond light
across the lawn. Surely, from the street,
he would have sensed how she waited to see
him, how she would sit and wait there all night
in silhouette, cashmere, and rouge, one hand
in her lap, the other on the Pall Malls in her pocket.

Then, inside, she felt he had her in his pocket—
with each cigarette she shared, each light,
each kiss she brushed against his freckled hand.
But he suddenly stood, ran back to the street,
disappearing into the moonless night,
where no one in the house could see.

She told her mother, *I gave him a smoke to see
him through. He was getting a match from his pocket.*
But her mother swore he stood there that night—
bare, like a beeswax candle in the light,
as plain as day, right there on the street.
She saw it from the upstairs, stiff in his hand.

The girl cried with her face in her hand—
then her mother said, *Oh, so now I see,*
you don't believe me, but I'm fairly street-
wise, girl, I've always had to keep my pocket-
book safe. I know what's what in the light.
The girl held to her vision of a knight—

he must have had his hand in his pocket.
Her mother could not see him in the dim light,
past the hooded streetlamps, alone at night.

Unconfessed: Portrait of My Father

He saunters into the American Legion near the port
   with others in peacoats, dress whites, guzzles Rolling Rocks,
chain-smokes Pall Malls, laughs a little too loudly.
   He hears church bells above "All Shook Up"
on the jukebox, remembers his dad's '55 Buick
   —the one he nose-dived into a telephone pole—
the night he flung melted beeswax on the stained-glass windows
   of St. Aloysius, the lace-white smock on Sundays
he wore to serve the priest the chalice during mass—
   Father Wilhelm, whose breath smelled of sherry,
communion wafers, cigarettes. How in the sacristy
   Father would grip a boy's wrist, draw it beneath
his vestments toward his creased black trousers.
   The sailor, in penance, sleeps at night on the floor.

How the Forbidden Egg Was Lost

Circa 1955

A woman with frosted hair and spider veins around her nose owned a golden egg. "A gift from my Russian aunt," she told everyone, but in truth she had eased the egg from her own fallopian tubes. The day it slipped from her folds, the woman noticed that the still-warm egg was cracked. To hide the flaw, she kept the golden egg on an easel in the center of a shelf, as if it were a work of art. She forbade her daughter to touch the egg, so of course the girl fondled it whenever the woman left the room. One night while the woman slept, the girl crept to the bathroom with the egg cradled in her palm. She rolled the egg over her chest and thighs and pressed it to her pubic bone, as if the trinket could open up a dark place within her. But just as the shadows were poised to enter the light, the woman barged into the bathroom, catching the girl with the egg bulging beneath the elastic of her underwear. The woman stuck her manicured fingers into the girl's panties, snatched the egg, and threw it down the laundry chute where it lay among the dirty linens. The next day the egg tumbled out of a damp pillowcase while the girl was hanging the sheets out to dry in the morning sun. It nestled in the grass like an Easter egg. Some days after the Harvest Moon, a squirrel buried the golden egg near the exposed roots of an oak, and then the snows came.

Last Lollipop

That night my aunts, all three in black serge,
crowded me up the attic stairs like a silent choir
to my great grandmother's attic bedroom.
Ana Penyak, the Kind Grandma from Slovakia,
the one who gave me toothless kisses,
lay on a cot under a sloped ceiling.
Wrapped in a green blanket, she was a caterpillar,
her head on a pillow—a baked apple with hair.
Ana stared, her eyes like crinkled cellophane.
She sucked on a butterscotch lollipop
clutched between bone of thumb and index.
There was a whole box of Russell Stover's
on the nightstand, but it wasn't the right time
to ask for one. Aunt Camilla nudged me—
Kiss her goodnight—and I obeyed,
brushing my lips against Ana's forehead.
On the way downstairs, my aunts clucked
their tongues about Ana only wanting sweets.
At daybreak, sun leaked under the roll-down shade
as the aunts called me from sleep—
the Kind Grandma had turned her face to the wall,
decided not to wake up. I hoped
the taste of butterscotch lasted her till morning.

Adventure-Land Kiddie Train in July

High up, on this still day, we sway inside the car,
stalled midway across a trestle. My mother's dark eyes
are round and shiny, like two black checkers pieces.
I tug at my red knit top, pull it away from my chest.

She blinks, grips the edge of the bench, hard.
"Be still," she says. A cloud drifts past the trees.
             "Where has your father gone to?"
In this train, a real but tiny train, we feel very small.

We could sailor-dive into the sea of treetops below.
We could hang by our shorts from branches, crack
our skulls against the iron trunks of elms.
             We could hold our breath.

Through the pane-less window I see a chain of men
growing along the trestle, hugging the forest-green cars.
And then a thick arm, grizzled with black hair,
not my father's, grabs me across the chest, lifts.

A man. He grips me close to his damp shirt, passes me
down the line to the other men, until the last one drops me
on the trampled grass. Where they held me tight, I'm sore.
I smell of sweat and engine grease, Old Spice and fear.

Illinois, 1973

They fluttered across newspapers like black
and white flags, smiles ready for the camera,
hair combed nice for yearbook picture day.
But this was summer, and thirteen girls lay in
cornfields and culverts, their bikes without riders,
wheels left spinning in the grass. Our legs
dangled with other legs at Pioneer Park pool,
blue anemones under dandelion suns,
our wrists wrapped with silver bracelets
stamped with names and numbers of POWs—
boys we imagined would someday love us.
Hot Tamale geraniums grew in time-lapse
stillness in my mother's window boxes
while we sat on the stoop and played jacks,
something about Watergate droning from inside,
something about bringing home the troops.
My mother's fingers, delicate as blades of grass,
pruned spent blossoms when she spoke to me.
Once she whispered about ovaries, hair
and other secret places. She told me
to come home before dark, but I never would listen.
Cracked sidewalk moons continued to rise;
we'd roller skate on sidewalks, the bells
clanging us home for supper out of earshot.
One night an owl called a single gospel note,
bats radioed from elm to elm, and a man
rolled his window down, inched past us,
a grin smeared under his nose, pants unzipped.
And then I did pedal home, pumping hard
down side streets to get away. Like a news flash
I saw their faces and wondered if, like me,
the dead girls went riding alone in the dark.

Learning to Pray in Spanish

Secrets cling to her like a damp sheet.
    It's summer on the Chattahoochee,
and July currents wrap silver arms
    around the rocks. Clay-stained
eddies tempt her to the riverbanks,
    to slip beneath the surface.
Is anyone looking down on her
    as she swims with Jesús in the sun?
He says, "Two hawks in the sky mean love,
    three hawks will bring bad luck."
Padre, Hijo, Espíritu Santo.
    Hot stone dries their backs
as they lie face up, fingers laced,
    counting hawks above the pines.

Pot smoke drapes them like a gauzy sheet
    where they hide by the Chattahoochee.
Jesús wraps her in his arms
    in the back seat of his clay-stained
Impala, in the woods near the banks.
    He presses words against her ear and she traces
his back with her fingertips—
    Princesa, bella, preciosa.
His mouth tastes like fast-moving currents.
    Padre, Hijo, Nuestra Señora.
They're behind a curtain of sumac, watching light
    swirl through the haze, gossamer shafts
cutting crisscross through the trees.
    Smoke-high kisses, the clear shimmer of water.

Her long hair drapes them like a silk sheet
    under the trees by the Chattahoochee.
Men fish in silence, not lifting their arms
    or turning to see who's there. Her clay-stained
sneakers mark the path near the banks.
    She lifts her face to the breeze.

"What's the word for most high?"
  Dios, Señor, Padre, Hijo.
Something about the spindly pines,
  the clouds, the burnt-sienna needles
and bark chips littering the path,
  the rocks, the blood-red ravines, are charms
against dim kitchens waiting for them
  at sunset, when they each leave for home.

Kudzu covers power lines in sheets
  on the roads near the Chattahoochee.
She slides close to Jesús, their arms
  touching as he drives down oil-stained
streets, away from the root-tangled riverbanks,
  to somebody his mother knows.
"What about Jesus, Mary and Joseph?"
  Jesucito, la Virgencita y todos los santitos.
A gray-haired doctor presses the pear
  inside her, helps her up from the table,
his hand still warm from her innards—
  "You're just six weeks along—it's not too late."
Clutching the paper gown closed,
  she covers her face with one hand.

A storm tears through leaves in sheets
  and pockmarks the Chattahoochee.
Behind the wheel, Jesús crosses his arms,
  almond eyes brackish. Grief stains
her cheeks with mascara, and the banks
  overflow above the tree roots.
Angel de la guarda—pray for me.
  The mud-brown river covers the shoals
where they sunbathed in July. Hail
  pings the roof, and "Stairway to Heaven"
whines on the radio. When the rain slows,
  she swings the door shut, waits. His car rolls up the hill.
And she imagines—right where she wants it to be—
  a hawk above the river, lifting a snake past the trees.

II. Story of Faults Concealed

Story of Faults Concealed

Our first date was a flyweight boxing match
I can't recall, only the veil of snow
flying with the wind under the streetlamps,
snow falling on his dark mustache, his mouth,
the cold kiss as we waited for the train.
An ivory globe of light around his hair
glowed like the Christmas Eve we met, when lamps
traced the gold in his cable-knit sweater.
Maybe the snow-veiled lights made some magic,
so that later, when he began to doubt me
and went to tell his worries to a priest,
I knew he would not ever try to leave.
He never saw me in as pure a light
as when those lamps were lit, after the fight.

Siesta at Hotel *La Sirena*

After the gazpacho, bacalao, and Rioja,
we seek the semi-darkness of our room.
The Roman window opens to a courtyard,
six stories high. When we first hear her,
I'm in a nightgown, the blanket pulled
to my chin, in bed with sudden chills,
a taste of medicine in my mouth. Sean
says, "Oh, a moaner," but he can't stay away
from the window. What a show, I think.
No one likes it that much. At five o'clock
her thick sounds wane, and he leaves
for the Crystal Palace to see Guernica,
in Spain for the first time since the war.

On fevered sheets I sleep through sunset
but roll over as her wails again fill the air.
I pat empty space on his side of the bed,
wonder if he's at a bar with a glass of beer,
slender in his hand, and think of her mirrored
above me on her double bed, same carved headboard,
same chairs studded with brass nails.
When I creep to the sink for water,
her cries travel up and down the bathroom pipes.
Outside, in the courtyard, shadows drape
over each sill in the moonlight—
men, drunk on her serenade, lean into the night.
Her song echoes, drifts into their mouths,
trickling down their parched, prosaic throats.

Pain Drives by the Delivery Room at Wayside Hospital

Propped up on a bed, knees open like books,
    heels braced, the doctor slides a tool
        like a knitting needle inside me.

Pain shifts into second gear, a churning engine
    at the base of my spine that revs
        from my throat in a plume of exhaust.

Pain is Rudolph Valentino in a silent movie—
    he won't take no for an answer. He hooks
        an arm around my middle and drags me

down a highway that knifes across a blue-moon desert.
    Wolves echo between cliffs. We surge
        around an S-curve, pain commanding me to push,

siphoning my baby's crown toward concrete.
    I lift my head—a metallic odor.
        Someone wipes blood from my thighs.

Pain rolls to a stop, drops me off. As I stumble
    along the road, headlights burn a halo
        across my vision. Gravel digs into my bare feet.

A dry wind flaps the hospital gown against
    the back of my legs. Leaning forward on the bed,
        I take hold of you. Afterbirth streaks your hair feathers.

Your eyes, two pools of black water.

Between Loads of Laundry

The struggle itself toward the heights is enough to fill a man's heart. One must imagine Sisyphus happy.
—*Albert Camus*

O this basket of towels at my feet,
   the same beige towels from last week,
      I fold and stack in the linen closet.

Against the terrycloth nap I run my fingers,
   forget what I'm doing,
      remember the Parade of Twins.

We are drinking chilled wine at a sidewalk café,
   the sky a veil of warmth;
      parents push matching daisies in strollers,

double blondes ride high in Cadillacs,
   and pairs of Mamie Eisenhowers dance
      to "The Time Warp," tapping with metal walkers.

Like glossy stallions two hearses roll by
   and then a gossamer Holy Spirit
      who floats among us on stilts.

After the parade we two-step in the street
   with fire-eaters, jugglers, contortionists.
      Through the floorboards I hear

the muffled timer buzzing in the basement.
   As I shut the linen closet door, a whoosh of air
      carries the scent of fabric-softener lilacs.

Day Trips

I play a mental listing game, a day
dream, no need to handle what's in the dark:
dragons drawn in crayon the boys made
now collecting dog hair under the bed,
toy sabers I hid (too sharp), my sons' dream-
world of sword play that took the shape
of samurais and khans. My inner eye shapes
the box where I keep photos of summer days
in Spain when we hadn't yet dreamed
the shadows under our eyes would darken,
Sean's snapshots of bullfights—one bull embedded
a horn in the matador's groin and made
him flop like a sock monkey—or did I make
that part up? Duffy and Red are shaped
like coiled rope at the foot of the bed.
I open a Moleskine to yesterday:
Driving car from backseat. Dark
up-do. Bride of Frankenstein. Dream-
scapes from last night. I think dreams
must filter through mattresses to rest in make-
shift coffins, sifting through some dark
terrain to reenter the mind, like the unshapely
woman with serpentine hair who day-
trips in my car while my body sleeps in bed.
Laura said in ten years' time our beds
double in weight from dead skin. My dreams
gather inside me, like motes in a noonday
shaft of light. At five o'clock I loll on unmade
sheets, sketch Sean's sweaters, misshapen
torsos draped across the footboard. I darken
in their folds until the sweaters' dark
wool blends with the dogs' fur and the bed
frame. In these shadows it's hard to tell one shape-
shifter from another—bulls, dragons, dreams
of backseat drivers, that troublemaker
who steers my car by night, sleeps by day.

Winterlight

Slanted rays warp the chlorine pool—
the crunch of acorns under foot and tire,
the distant sun, and a dull ache have ripened
my desire to swim these laps indoors.
You are a phantom who flutter kicks
my crawl along the black-line tiles,
and I weep into my goggles, freestyle.
As I glide through water air-bubble slick,
I conjure back our August constellations,
Venus and Vega overhead, pretend I
haven't missed your crooked mouth, a lie—
winter's pale planets can't be unspun.
But by swimming this, I distill some pain,
these floating whorls of light what now remain.

Bombed

The moon rises, a corpse on a butter-turned sky
above ragged curtains of pine. I've buried you
a hundred times behind the toolshed,
and still you kick my head like a Cossack.
How I want you to shoot, how you shoot me up good,
how you send me to la-la land just in the nick of time,
how you scorch me with your chipped-ice mouth,
how you light up my position. You're my infrared.
A strategic engagement, our sparkle in the basement,
but you end up bunched between my knees
when I hide you in brown bags, plastic water bottles.
Were we ever in cahoots like I thought we were?
Clouds tarnish the moon and blur the trees.
Carpenter bees scratch the eaves while I finish you off.

Wife's Aubade

Weekends, he stays upstairs past one,
blinds shut against the sun, the changing leaves.
He waits for me to wake him, and sometimes
I do, slipping out of T-shirt and jeans
to join him in our double bed.
As we fold in a body-length caress,
our sadness rises like the smell of fresh bread
diffused throughout the house,
traces left on curtains, tables, chairs.
But today I turn from his rhythmic breaths—
today he's another sink of dishes that weighs
on my breastbone like a wide river rock.
And while our house lifts and settles in sleep,
I walk alone on leafy Sunday streets.

Psyche's Complaint to Eros

For Sean

I touch but never see your face.
If I even reach for the light,
you sift through darkness I can't trace,

my hands left raking empty space.
I hold you only by moonlight—
a touch, but not the sight of your face,

screened behind this carapace
of shadows. Toward some height
you unspool without a trace,

like the deep quiver of a bass
violin or pulsing bats in flight.
We touch but never turn to face

each other in this blinded place.
Stay with me till daylight,
or leave a clue for me to trace.

Slanted rays and wingbeats efface
the edges of our sun-pinked night.
Just when I almost see your face,
you fade, *sotto voce*, leave no trace.

Losing It

I've lost the one with with a pea-green circle and a capital *B* for Balance,
the center where I practiced a science
of jumps that wring the body in 90 minutes.
We'd stretch flat, salty on our slick mats, synapses steamed,
and the teacher would place towels soaked in lavender over our eyelids.
And though we'd chant *Om* and my nerves would uncoil,
in the night cogs would turn in my chest
until one August morning, when the moon was high,
I curled like a fist around a lily.
You brought me to a clinic whose prints of cherry blossoms
and snow-peaked mountains said, *Calm down, have faith.*
The doctor wagged his index finger before my eyes,
a lone windshield wiper slapping the rain, his trick
to prepare my mind for the command: *You will relax.*
When I hiccuped in terror, he said, *You're not trying hard enough.*
He gave me a a blue pill for sleep and a pink pill for time-released results,
but I woke in the night with an urge to dance out the window.
You found me, smoothed my hair, convinced me I wasn't dying.
And after days of ironing, listening to *The Artist's Way,*
and long walks while the world was at school,
the capsules softened me, the way a little Vaseline on a lens blurs the focus,
and I napped on the couch for two weeks in my favorite T-shirt,
the one with a *B* for Balance, the one I've lost,
the one that barely touches my skin, it's that light.

If Only

I had told you sooner about the doctor's tobacco-stained
sibilants brimming over his baleen teeth,
the spells sifting through his mustache,
how he'd pull on his pipe and eye me like a spider,
spinning nicotine threads to trap me at his feet.
I hadn't waited ten thousand minutes
before your face blanched in grief's cracked mask.

Dissociation in June

Home from the night shift, the naugahyde couch
receives him. Superheroes litter the rug.

At first he refuses to believe. Our sons
are building Lego spaceships in their room.

"I won't be going to therapy anymore."
He doesn't want to know. I sit close to him.

Birds are landing on the deck to eat leftover toast.
Sunlight is hitting the pines out back.

"You should stop going to him, too."
"I can't," he says, "I'm part of the group."

Crows fly into the trees. A squirrel scratches the roof.
From my mouth I let drop the words to tell him—

took, advantage, and *touched* fall on the floor.
His face blanches, cracks. I take our boys to the front yard.

Sunlight illuminates spent azalea blossoms
yellowing the wide crescent of lawn.

In the blue plastic wading pool float dead wasps.
The boys try to spill the wasps, but the plastic won't give.

He comes out of the house and starts the car.
He asks Dylan, "You want to drive?"

He sets our four-year-old on his lap, lets him steer.
They turn around at the Bamboo Forest.

Casey says, "If everyone tries, we can empty it," and so we do.
All four of us go to one side of the pool and lift.

Water spills onto dark green blades of grass
that, in the morning light, gleam as if coated in glass.

III. Confidentiality

Countertransference

At our first meeting, a Wednesday, Dr. X
held my hand in his, said, *Enjoy your rest*
at the lake, breathe fresh air, go for a swim.
In a month you'll be seeing in color.
In a month I returned, a Wednesday. He shook
hands with me again, prolonged his grasp, said,
I was not prepared for this loveliness.
Illumined in front of a paned glass door,
he stared at me, smoking a scented pipe.
My back to the glass, I saw him brightened—
the sun on his mustache, the baleen-like
teeth that emerged when he smiled, the light
in his olive, hooded eyes that lingered
a few beats too many. His menthol breath
came in hot puffs. I took his fixation
the wrong way. I thought he meant to cure me.

Prescribed

She counts out pills for seven days,
in equal measures of blue and green,
then places them in plastic trays.

She tells herself, "It's just a phase.
This year I'll start a new routine."
She counts out pills for seven days

in quiet rooms, her mind a maze.
Eying each pill like a jellybean,
she places them in plastic trays.

Her guru orders healing sprays
of heated water and histamine.
She counts out pills for seven days,

does Hatha yoga and deep pliés.
The magic number—just fourteen—
she places in their plastic trays.

If chanting mantras cleared this haze,
she'd flush the lot and live serene.
She counts out pills for seven days,
then places them in plastic trays.

Lament

How I was hit, how I still propel forward,
    how the functions of my body will soon end,
    how the slight stain of blood has returned
from the dry darkness of inner cavities, the chance
    I could still conceive, the certainty I never will again,
    concrete towers crusting the landscape, bits of trash
mixed in the grass along the access ramp, praying mantis
    streetlights peering over the ten-lane highways,
    dumpsters graffitied with tags I'll never decipher,
the woman in a tank top who stands between lanes
    in the nighttime rain with no umbrella, oncoming
    traffic splashing the jeans plastered to her legs,
how her face, like layers of wet leaves, shines
    in the headlights, her arms iced branches held out for dollar bills,
    how I make sure the doors are locked,
how I don't lower my window to give her some cash,
    how it's dark and cold and I don't want to get soaked.

Letter of Conciliation to Dr. X

Buddha says we've been at this many times,
    and by this I mean these lives we've lived before,
        reweaving our patterns of crisscrossed lines.

We get it right, or we switch back for more
    of the same, and with the same people, too.
        Different bodies, the same uneven score.

I'd like to disrupt this pattern with you,
    change the threads of our cosmic tapestry.
        If you think of me at all, you should do

likewise—amend our ancient history.
    Could I have crushed you ten lifetimes ago,
        erstwhile villain, galactic enemy?

May we learn from *this* what we need to know
to swim our way clear of fate's undertow.

Father Xavier Seduces the Merchant's Wife

His eyes are glowing like church votives.
Incense swirls through his beard.
"Undress," he says, and I do.
He strips his rank monk's robe,
his chest crosshatched with hair and grime,
but his eyes won't break that light
he sends me, icons only he can decipher.
His onion stench turns to sandalwood,
and he says, "Resist me," but those flames—
I want to slip him a coin for a prayer,
not for the poor, but for me.
We lie on a stone floor, a sack of potatoes
molding in the corner, but his eyes,
two crystal rosary beads, convince me
we tangle in a field of lavender,
that God himself burns this halo around his head.

Mechanical Age

As she grinds her hips on the dew-wet ground,
a wife writes in her journal, June 1900.
They say she has hysterics, astray in thought,
but hasn't she gone to see Dr. Xavier
who used a magic wand to medicate?—
a new and improved pelvic massage for ladies.
He shut the door, told her to lie down,
fold your hands, close your eyes, but she peeked
as he undraped his mechanical instrument
and she felt the engine, steam-driven, pile-driven,
Lord God in heaven, hallowed be thy name!
But it was all the same for Xavier.
He merely stopped to wipe his brow
when she hitched up her underskirt and lowed.

Hippocratic Oath

Normal is a setting on a dryer, he said,
and should-hood is shit-hood, remember that.
Listen, you're living in your head,

all filled up with that tripe you've read
about men in frock coats and silk cravats.
Normal is a setting on a dryer, he said.

Don't take no for an answer in bed—
learn how to give and take a love pat.
You know, you're living in your head.

Wear a dress that can raise the dead
the next time you come for our chat.
Normal is a setting on a dryer, he said,

so do what you want. Morality's dead.
Look in the mirror. You're getting fat.
If you're not living in your head,

baby, my name isn't Dr. Xavier DuBled.
Come sit next to Papa—this is where it's at.
Normal is a setting on a dryer, he said.
Listen, you're living in your head.

Tour of a Cloister Near Salamanca, 1910

A mound of bulbs blossoms in a veil of light
under the convent stairwell, a chiaroscuro
of damp and dusty skulls. Sister Pius, our guide,
says, *The crypt, for nuns entered for life.*
Her face crimps around her wimple
and a breeze moves her stiff black habit
as we climb to a walkway along the outer walls.
Grass bends over stones pocking the field.
She points beyond the crumbling battlements—
Where that bull grazes lies Xavier, a surgeon
who sliced out young girls' wombs, his butcher's cure
for palsied nerves. Rescued by her brothers,
one girl then took her vows. They tossed Xavier
to the crows. Her bones rest in our sacred bed.

The Czarina Defends Father Xavier

Dust in his beard, smut under his nails,
misspelled letters smeared with a greasy fist.
Little Father, Little Mother, he calls us.
No matter. When these prayers dart like crows
over rooftops, he'll cork the vodka.
When he hears my muffled wails
flooding the halls, to reach my son's side
he'll peel away the whore and ride his mare
till she's more than spent. The laying on
of dark hands. Staunch the seeping, Father—
help me say the words—of blood. Father
Xavier, come like an owl, lift the rats
off my baby, spit their clotted pellets in the fields.
Only then will I take to my rooms and sleep.

Confidentiality

A mahogany desk, lamps with terra-cotta
bases and amber shades, two love seats
upholstered in paisley, his musky cologne,
his walrus mustache, the bow tie,
the starched dress shirt, the wool jacket,
how he lit his pipe with a wooden match,
how he handed me tissues when the tears came.
Who can explain why I missed the essentials?
Was it the residue of sleepless nights
or the string of days when I couldn't choke
down a spoonful of soup? It remains a fact—
I failed to observe there was no license
to practice framed on the wall, only a Georgia
O'Keefe he claimed the artist gave him.

IV. Suburban Llorona

After Dark Llorona

She will swoop from the clouds
in a white gown edged in antique lace,
cackling, crying her lost loves,
her bony fingers riffling the grass
near the muddy riverbanks.
Her black hair, wild as willows,
will switch your face if you pass,
and if you wade even to your shins
she will twine you in her hair,
drag you by your ankles, and—
silt against scalp, grit between teeth—
you will flail downriver, to a river below
the river, darker than anthracite,
colder than salts dripping off stalactites.
She will crack your ribs, your eyes
straining like fish eggs in a membrane.
If you could breathe, you would wail
Mother, I am not your child.

Colonial Llorona

In some stories she polished the parquet floors
    and engraved shields of a *criollo* lord
who plied her with sherry and sugared dates
    she carried on trays in the evening.
From his high bed, in chamois breeches, he woos her
    to his side and, of course, she bears his child
and then another. Some say she tried to trap him,
    but noblemen seldom marry the maid.
When he sails for Spain in search of a gilded bride,
    she wraps the babies in her apron folds
and heaves them, like stones, into the river.
    Later, her dress bells as she hangs from a rope swing
tied to a branch. And then she lets go, a muslin
    blossom, till the water's weight draws her down.

Rio Grande Llorona

Ranchers say she tended bar and cavorted with men
    while her small sons dreamed of giants.
Tonight, home from her shift, she scans the empty cots,
    the open window and the path below
branching toward river and town. In this tale,
    her boys have walked in sleep to the river.
She runs, slapping through mud and reeds, only to rest
    her hands on quiet chests under a quilt
of water. Thrashing the currents, stripped to her slip,
    she pulls at her long hair. All through the night
she weeps for their breath to rise with the morning mist:
    Sweet sons, sweet sons, listen to me, sweet sons.
Even still, we hear her plea hissing in the rapids
    as the river rushes past us to the sea.

Clermont Lounge Llorona

Off highways, in diners, there's talk she has appeared.
    Some young guy, let's call him Jason, stumbles
far from wife and home, unable to resist the bars
    where dancers swim their arms through sour smoke,
glow-strips taped around their tattooed breasts.
    Onlookers say Jason elbowed toward the musk
and patchouli oils of a woman to his left
    and reached to touch the tips of her long hair,
unprepared for the sudden shock, then fear,
    as she spun her horse-skull jaw to face him,
jabbing his Adam's apple with some claw or hoof,
    ice where he would have wished her eyes to be.
Her tongue, quick as any cobra's, bleats a danger
    he can't decode as he lies, breathless, on the floor.

Suburban Llorona

In this picket-fence version of the tale she does
    marry the man, and together they raise
their sons in the shadows of fig trees and ivy.
    She nurses her babies with brackish milk,
rinses their dirty diapers with her dripping brine,
    and stirs tears into soup instead of salt.
In her grief, she believes in a doctor who claims
    he's bishop, rabbi, shaman, dean, who boasts
that he's the only one to staunch her seeping eyes.
    He fixes her by swaying a gold watch
and towels up her tears by putting her to sleep.
    When she wakes, she discovers the house has flooded.
Her husband watches TV on the roof,
    their sons adrift, far out somewhere on makeshift rafts.

Malinche's Curse

Aztec shamans gifted twenty virgins
to bearded men approaching on the waves

because this holy apparition swelled
like their plumed serpent, Quetzalcoatl.

What better way to enter heaven than
multiple unions with a fertile god?

Among the brides the tribesmen offered up
was *la Malinche,* who knew some secret words

she bartered to couple with their king—
frijoles, tomate, chocolate, maíz.

Orozco paints her as the blood-red Eve
Cortés held down with conquistador arms,

though Rivera dresses her in dahlia white
and ties a blue-eyed baby to her back.

See how the little mother bows her head,
faceless, in back with the soldiers and mules.

Coatlicue, Aztec Mother of the Gods

December 21, 2012

We hear her mournful calls from far away,
so far we can't remember why she left
or who she was, or why she didn't stay.
The timber of her voice says she's bereft:

Oh my children, how will I ever find you?—
her question clamors in a thundercloud.
Or she cries, when will I ever hold you?
And in our fear we leave the fields unplowed.

Some think that she will lift us to the sun,
a western heaven where the corn grows thick.
They pray for her to heal them with homespun
songs, to purge their demons, to cure the sick.

Others think she comes to end our days—
she'll hook us in her claws but leave no mark.
Snakes for a skirt, jawbone pale, she brays
the omens of our sleep in endless dark.

Lamia Speaks, Mother to Mother

How could a mother's gullet take her living child?
    You'd never, *could* never eat your own child,
not even if God himself pried apart your lips.
Imagine chopping peppers, stirring butter beans,
    heeding some green, green urge to add the flesh
of your flesh, the tender little bits, to the stew.
Tie a silver amulet around your daughter's neck.
    Tell your cares to rag dolls you tuck into
her pocket. When crows caw at sunrise, cross yourself.
    Hold them back from creeks where, a cottonmouth,
I've slipped from Spanish moss and low-hanging branches.
Revenge afflicts the one who seeks it—I should know.
    At night I pop my eyes onto a plate;
even a demon longs for whitewashed, dreamless sleep.

Frida Kahlo's Blue House

In her home, now a museum, hangs a floating fetus
painting, collage of grief and loss.

The guide points out the names of Diego's lovers
traced in blood-red cursive along the borders of her bedroom wall.

They've made refrigerator magnets of her self-portrait
with Diego in her arms, nursing like a baby at her breast.

She called him beloved toad.
Whose beloved were you, Frida?

She shot back tequila and smoked to dull the pain
of a spine, a heart, held together with staples, barbed wire.

Her corset was a plaster cast painted with roses and poppies,
a vase for delicate shoulders.

She gave herself nightingale eyebrows,
black wings of mercy lifting her skyward.

Did you get what you wanted?

Men carried her, Cleopatra in a litter, to her last exhibit.
She was forty-seven that night she arrived, on her deathbed.

Eve Clears Her Garden

Spring forced no life from the apple tree
so we took it down, dragging crown and trunk
to the yard for the boys to chop into logs.
Then the soil—taproots thick as wrists, severed
with pickax and machete, rocks and clay
loosened with tines of hoe and pitchfork. Leaves,
sheaves of them bleaching under this year's
brown ones, peeled away. Worms slid through sleek mud
as blade tips carved nearby. From a tide
of mulch, pale as a sprig of thyme, a snake
flashed its stripes like a dart, and I dropped the spade.

There is flawless blue where the tree
once reached. Verbena and asters now pink
the hill instead of old geometries,
those leafless branches. A sphinx moth, some kind
of flying serpent, takes wary sips from
rose, then phlox, then flies in my direction,
as if to reach the pith of me and my temptation.
The urge is to coax seedlings into vines,
to answer the call of minstrel goldfinch,
to open my throat's hive and free the bees
that seem to buzz between each breath, each rib.

Postcard Madonna

After detail of El Greco's La Sagrada Familia

What you see is my face encircled in a psychedelic nimbus,
jet-black hair held in place under a lace mantilla, eyes downcast,
skin like cream, lips and robes stained the color of ripe berries.
What you don't see is the infant held to my breast,
his fingers entwined with mine. I would show him to you,
but he's been cropped from my story. He's soil, cosmic dust, words on a page.
Call me *Mare*, for North Star, for bitter seas, for unshed tears.

Buddhist Proverb

In memory of the Atlanta Child Murders, 1979-1981

The dead are many, the living few.
So many have lost a brother, or a friend.
Thin ropes of rain strike the roof
as she waits for her son to come home.

So many have lost a brother, or a friend.
She parts a curtain, looks into the dark
and waits for her son to come home—
he walked down to Leon's Bottle Shop.

She parts a curtain, looks into the dark—
a neighbor saw him cross Elm Street.
He walked down to Leon's Bottle Shop
and tipped over the edge of night.

A neighbor saw him cross Elm Street.
He went to buy her a tin of snuff
and just tipped over the edge of night.
Or did some spirit whisk him away

after he bought her the tin of snuff?
Maybe he's gone to his father's house.
Did some spirit whisk him away,
through the pines down by the creek?

Maybe he's gone to his father's house.
Thin ropes of rain strike the roof.
Among the pines down by the creek,
the dead are many, the living few.

Rusted Chains

In your car I find lighters, eye drops,
an empty baggie. I sniff the residue.

Plant particles filter through sunlight,
disappear onto my lap.

On a timeline of frames along a wall
you appear in a homemade astronaut suit

holding a ball in the Heisman stance,
pushing chest first into the wind,

your eyes shaped like my own but darker,
like a coal mine, a new-moon midnight.

You worried you wouldn't be good enough,
secretly wanting to be the star.

You were once a secret star growing inside me.
A winter morning in Georgia—

We're swaying on a wooden swing
suspended from the branch of a live oak.

You are eleven months old—Crayola-green snowsuit,
nursing al fresco. You fall asleep in my arms.

Wispy black hair blowing around your face.
Lashes feathering Cream of Wheat skin.

I freeze-frame the moment under the soft December sun.
The chains creak as we rock together.

Artist at 18

As morning sneaks through porch screens, splays
across dog-chewed wicker chairs and woven rugs,
my son reaches over jars of daylilies for his plate of eggs.
Between mouthfuls he says Chloe wants him
to leave early, to reach their condo before night.
Gold-blonde, green-eyed sylph, she wears cherry-
red halter tops, braids friendship bracelets from her big toe,
sings "La Vie en rose" in perfect French,
gives him gifts of chai, Pablo Neruda, macaroons.
He looks at the floor, long hair hiding his face,
and mentions her family's marble tiles, Picasso
lithographs, intaglio prints, her brother's friends
with their casual tans, flipped collars, BMWs.
"Those guys would take her for granted," I say.
"You couldn't teach me to treat her bad," he says.

Later, packing linseed oil and paints, he shows me
the canvas he'll finish in Pensacola—I see what could be
an eye flashing through storm-churned waves,
magma glowing on a mountain crag, a brush fire
riding a wheat field, flames spilling over the frame—
a landscape he arrived at, he says, by accident.

Cruel Aprils

Into our view shouldered the funnel cloud.
No time to consider options, the mothers
followed commands to flee the windowed gym,
to crouch under cinderblocks in a mass
while their boys came running in from the field.

My son refused to climb into the van
with the coach and his team. He had to find me,
to keep me from the storm, and when he did,
we thought we were safe.
                                        His team, the Thunder.
His number—23—his birthdate, his grandfather's,
great-grandfather's too, significant facts
we know but don't yet fathom, not even
why his dad was born on Valentine's Day,
spoiling the karmic balance by nine days.

A decade later, hail has stripped dogwoods
of blossoms. Again the lid to our house
has lifted with thunderclouds. Wind has spit
nails into the cracked sky and rain ticktocks
its Dada metronome on our bowed heads.

From where I sit cross-legged on the rug,
I reach an arm to the rafters and shut
the roof, but the molding is no longer flush.

Sonnet for a Song Maker

You say you know your Self outside of time,
    a meeting that arises with two words:
I AM. My firstborn son, these bells you chime,
    these chords you strum that ride the air like birds
among the leaves and branches of your thought...
    I trust you've tapped the wellspring of your song,
but sometimes still your frets and strings go taut,
    as if the notes you chose were somehow wrong.
I've seen the clash of cymbals in your eyes
    and sensed the drums that roll within your brain.
Perhaps these chanted madrigals are cries
    composed from missing parts of the refrain—
I AM ENOUGH, a different verse to sing,
    three words that echo with an altered ring.

Philosopher at Twenty-two

He reads *Madness and Civilization* under fluorescent lights,
as if the book were a sun and he the plant,

but he suddenly stands, passes others looped over laptops,
and moves into September night.

On Moreland he buys a coffee, and a dusty girl in dreadlocks
holds out a hand for the cup—he gives it, and she sings

Hey! Mr. Tambourine Man, play a song for me
as he glides down the street toward the train.

Then the flames rain on his head, his rib cage
a kind of combustion—even now the warmth simmers

in the space between his eyebrows.
A creature descended upon him that night,

not as in a vision, but an alien force, a demiurge,
an angel come to scourge him of delusions.

Today my son wears frayed T-shirts, cut-offs, sandals,
beard grazing lip and chin.

He has been one of them for a time,
tuned in to their frequencies, waves he begins to interpret.

Number 1, 1948

At Thanksgiving my freshman son unfurls
his sails—collages of plastic babies
tagged @99cents, bees swirling from
constellations of skulls, narratives
scoured from Baltimore's blown-out buildings.

He says the first time he pinned his work to the board
a girl remarked, "These drawings look
like somebody locked himself in a room
and painted his ravings on the walls."

Later we go to the High, and I admit
a preference for Matisse's domestic interiors,
tracing his wallpaper to some logical conclusion,
that Pollock leaves me tense, out of breath;
and he asks, "How do you feel about Number 1, 1948?"
                              "Angry," I say.
But when we turn to Pollock's black dribbles
we track one of his dodecaphonic arcs, and together
we drift toward a handprint, an anchor
at the edge of this kinesthetic sea.

After Reading *Winesburg, Ohio*

In this loosely conceived plot, I latched onto the truth of the mother
    whose son won't become a man until she dies.
She plastered freedom into a hole behind the bed—
    mad money for her son, though all he needed
was her zeal to fade along with her withering body.
    Siddhartha's mother died a week after his birth,
Moses had to float the Nile in his orphan's boat
    to hear the fire speak, and Christ was the Son of Man
before the angel touched his mother in a dream.
    My son burned his truth into me with his black eyes
at the kitchen table. He said he comes from heaven,
    that he is dope, and I must forget him. I should get over him
like a girl gets over her first heartbreak. Miles away,
    a train sounds in the dark. He will follow its call, *Woman, trust me.*

Swimming Stockbridge Bowl

Into dark water, I swim toward the island
    away from my son on the floating dock
where he suns his blemished chest.
    Wind on my face, sound of breath,
smell of stone-green lake.
    Low in the sky, an arrow of geese.
There's an element of faith when
    we migrate far from shore that we'll keep
the markers stored somewhere—
    the lake's curve near the spruce, the white buoy,
my son on the dock, signs that tell me
    I'm on the right path. I've gone too far.
I know I could cramp, but now the island
    is just as close as the dock.
I approach boulders on the island's edge.
    A snail brushes against an arm.
Shallow-water weeds tangle in the heart
    my hands trace in dark-water breaststroke.
I circle back, full of the rush of deep lake,
    solitary frog-kick breath, dipping,
rising, catching the air,
    eyes trained on the blur of blue-gray
dock where my son waits.
    I climb the ladder, tip the dock.
He props on an elbow, lifts his gaze,
    says, "I watched till your red cap disappeared."

Gift After Crossing the Threshold

In Sarasota we saw boats as white as bleached bones
    docked in gray-green waves, the causeway to St. Armand's
        stretched like a giant mandible over the bay,

hotels like ivory chess pieces, and ibises,
    flocks of them, with delicate, curved necks, poking
        around the surf at dusk, legs lime-green in the October sun.

When we returned, I found a dead bird on the threshold.
    It lay as if in stiff sleep, face covered with a leaf,
        its feathers the same green as the ibis legs.

I was afraid to touch a dead or injured animal,
    so Casey got the shovel from the garage, scooped
        up the bird, and flung it into the brambles out back.

He said maybe a turkey buzzard would eat it.
    Dylan said he wished we had saved the bird—
        we could have strung it by its neck from a branch

to let the flesh decay—he could have sketched the bones.
    Today I think, What Georgia bird has lime-green feathers?
        We didn't even know what kind of bird it was.

Now I rake through poison ivy and bamboo, tracing
    the invisible arc of the bird's catapulted corpse.
        But all I find are green shadows, some bits of gold

where sunlight breaks through dried-out summer leaves.
    It's not the bird I seek, but the bird's death,
        to see and touch the silent plumage as if it were my own.

We Wish This Enduring Body

After The First Study for the Madonna of Port Lligat

My tall son says, "Sometimes Dalí
    painted with a single strand of hair."
Then he drifts toward a geometric skull

and blends into the crowded hall.
    I turn back again to the Madonna,
painted in Gala's likeness. She floats

where the water merges with the sky.
    Her chest, hollow where one expects
sternum and ribs to enclose her heart,

is now a window to that calm sea.
    The land dissolves, the shoreline blurs.
The stillness of her blue air lulls me.

She half smiles on the hollowed child
    as he hovers over her lap, his gaze
fastened to a shadow on her white robes,

the shadow of a tiny cross he holds
    in his left hand, like a toy. Her crown
of gold hair is cleft in two, and I wonder—

Did anticipation of grief split her?
    She spires her hands over his fontanelle,
in spite of knowing. In the background,

cities, statues, towers crack and fall.
    What rises from this life intact, stepping
from a shell in a froth of breaking waves?

V. The Red Weaver

Self-portrait

Rain rips through fat tulip poplars.
    I'm reading on the couch while my son
        sketches my portrait: glasses, graying hair,

the neck lined but the torso still upright.
    Later I show him the pencil drawing TC
        made of me when we were in our twenties.

He admires the confident, quick lines,
    her attention to detail. I admire the contour
        of my jaw, the bright eyes, the hip's curve

where I sit with legs curled to the side,
    our cat Kazoo in my lap. "Strange," I say,
        "I still see myself that way." "Yes," he says,

"that would be strange." He's just seventeen.
    When the rain stops, I go out to get the mail
        but first inspect my face in the hall mirror—

shadows like splinters near the mouth, lank hair.
    The hummingbirds on the front porch
        clink when I linger to touch their glass circles.

Cobwebs have collected between the tines.
    I consider dusting them away, but the sun is out
        and beads of water in the webs catch the light.

Folly Beach

Wet sand near breakers reflects clouds, pale sky.
    I should be in heaven, but I'm not.
        I want someone to crack my heart open,
make it as wide as the beach
    beating in rhythm with the waves.

I think of the Buddhist monk called One Finger,
    Gutei Isshi, who answered questions about
        the Dharma by raising one finger, a silent signal,
I imagine, like the icons of St. John
    the Baptist gesturing toward God.

Gutei Isshi once cut off a student's finger
    to teach the boy a lesson. As the boy ran,
        clutching his fallen finger, One Finger
called to him. When the boy turned his head,
    One Finger pointed toward the sky.
        They say he stopped the boy's mind.

If Gutei Isshi strolled beside me,
    his saffron robes trailing in the surf,
        he'd reach his pointer finger
under my sternum, strum the aorta,
    pluck the ventricle, and then,
        with the curl of a digit, he'd dig out my heart
and fling it into the bottle-green waves.

What I want in place of a heart: a chest cavity
    as wide as the space between stars.

Pelicans skim the water for fish, gulls call,
    a toddler runs downshore from her mother,
        jellyfish spill on the wet sand, breezes
carry the scent of sea muck. In the heaven
    I desire, my skin dissolves in the salt air
        and the sun steams my skeleton to a mist.

Some Unrecognized and Unearthly Lover

After William Carlos Williams

Your crooked flower appeared in my dream
　　last night. Before sleep, I wrote in the margins
　　　　of my book how you had merged yourself

with the yellow petals of that single spray.
　　You said the blossom wasn't a mustard flower,
　　　　and I reasoned that to name the fleshy leaves

would spell the flower's end. I didn't dream
　　about yellow or gold. What came were words,
　　　　lyrics from books, and we all read and sang

them into some crowded room. And as we listened
　　to each other, I felt the contours of our bodies
　　　　begin to dissolve, and we blended together

as a dark, pulsing thing. But in the way
　　of dreams, the walls of the room also fell away
　　　　to long sidewalks shaded with live oaks

where I walked holding hands with someone
　　I loved when I was twenty, whose name
　　　　came to mind before I fell asleep.

Woman Buys Soul on eBay

ABC News, 2007

She might have seen that bid for six six six
and didn't want the soul to go to some devil
from the Badlands, the Mojave, or Scranton.

But how to collect? How long the wait?
Would she stand at the mailbox to receive her goods, hoping
the carrier would handle the package with care?
Would a man in brown stick a notice on her door?

Maybe she desired the magic that happens
when funds are transferred—the binary discharge,
the tumble of light from one account to another.

What if souls transmit through fiber optics?

She could drive by the bank to retrieve the spirit,
punch in her secret code, and catch the sparks
with a plastic ziplock, like a child bringing home a goldfish.

What if she funneled the contents into a decanter,
set the cut glass on the mantel,
waited for blues and golds to emerge from ether—

would the soul swim in circles for months
until it settled to the bottom, astral dust she might never see?

Perimeter Shopping Trip

After Au bonheur des dames, Remedios Varo

In a body made of cogs and wheels, riding the cusp
of cronehood, you think of lips stained berry-red that whisper
in the dark: Buy a new one, or you'll fade away.
You don't believe you're a doll, yet you act as if you were
made of styrofoam. You roll out the door
of your cuckoo-clock garage to line up with the others,
driving to the halls where mannequins model spare parts:
platinum teeth, rubber knees, silk noses, pinwheel eyes spinning
in perfumed mist. Arms, legs, a head reflect off black marble,
and the question arises—Whose face is that? Glass doors open and close.
The cool hush of air. Escalators ease you to the lower level.

Harmony

After Remedios Varo

She works like other alchemists,
alone in a dark room, eyes
half closed, listening. And if she hears
a chord, it might sound like water
dripping from pipes. Creaking floorboards,
thrumming walls, a distant train. Glass
clinking in cupboards. Rhythms take shape
as if she could touch their contours,
as if a crow's caw just outside the window
made the living bird beat in her hands.
Pigeons seem to pass through walls
at will. She can sense the tender brush
of wing feathers against her temples.

The Red Weaver

After Remedios Varo

In a corner of a dark room she winds
    a skein of rose-colored wool into a ball.
        Behind her graying crown of braids
fleur-de-lis on papered walls
    reflect their vague faces in the mirror,
        and from the open window—
fresh-cut grass, lavender, sweet basil
    pale evening sun, breezes.
        She breathes in the clear light
of being and shuts her eyes.
    She dreams the red scarf she will knit
        has gathered itself from her lap
and become a woman. Rose-colored hair,
    arms open like wings—poised to fly under the sash.
        She wakes in her chair, wonders where
the scarf woman has flown.
    The light in the room has faded.
        Yarn rubs across her fingers.
She casts on the first row.
    Through the glass, onto rose-colored walls,
        shadows and sunset shift like flames.

Notes

"Story of Faults Concealed" takes as its inspiration Shakespeare's "Sonnet 88."

Dr. Xavier is a fictitious character, a malevolent doctor and religious charlatan who appears throughout time in various guises. The line "A new and improved pelvic massage for ladies" comes from a 1910 newspaper advertisement titled "Vibration is Life."

"Father Xavier Seduces the Merchant's Wife" and "The Czarina Defends Father Xavier" allude to the relationship between the Romanov Czars and Grigori Yefimovich Rasputin, who was a spiritual advisor to Alexandra. She believed in his powers to heal her hemophiliac son. During the time Rasputin associated with the Romanov family, rumors were spread that he was having carnal relations with the Czarina, her daughters, and other women in her household.

"After Dark Llorona," "Rio Grande Llorona," "Colonial Llorona," "Diamond Club Llorona," and "Suburban Llorona" explore the southwestern myth of *La Llorona*, the Weeping Woman. *La Llorona* is a ghost-like figure who wanders riverbanks looking for her drowned sons. Urban legends have reported sightings of *La Llorona* in bars and on highways. Ethnologists and students of folklore have traced the Weeping Woman to La Malinche and the mesoamerican goddess Coatlicue. In almost all versions of the myth, she appears as a fallen woman who serves as a cautionary figure for children, men, and women who might consider straying from the social norms.

"Lamia Speaks Mother to Mother": Lamia was a beautiful Libyan queen who became a consort of Zeus, with whom she had several children. When Hera discovered their liaison, she cursed Lamia and caused the queen to devour her own children; as if this curse were not enough, she turned Lamia into a serpent who then killed and ate the children of other mothers.

"Some Unrecognized and Unearthly Lover" takes its title from a line in William Carlos Williams' poem "The Yellow Flower."

Acknowledgments

The author acknowledges, with thanks, the following journals in which these poems have appeared, sometimes in earlier versions.

Ouroboros Review: "Last Lollipop," "Between Loads of Laundry," "Pain Drives by the Delivery Room"
Blue Fifth Review, Blue Five Notebook: "The Red Weaver"
Red Clay Review: "Frida Kahlo's Blue House"
Naugatuck River Review: "Hotel La Sirena"
Hot Metal Bridge: "Harmony"
Flycatcher: "Learning to Pray in Spanish" (winner of the 2012 Agnes Scott Literary Festival Prize in poetry), "Folly Beach"
Tampa Review: "Perimeter Shopping Trip"
Slant, a Journal of Poetry: "Courtship, 1958"
Canopic Jar: "Adventure-Land Kiddie Train in July," "Self Portrait"
Out of Sequence: The Sonnets Remixed: "Story of Faults Concealed"
Peony Moon: "Hippocratic Oath"
Hobble Creek Review: "Woman Buys Soul on eBay"
Broad River Review: "Illinois, 1973" (Honorable Mention for the Rash Award in Poetry)
Birmingham Poetry Review: "Colonial Llorona," "Suburban Llorona"
The Mom Egg: "Number 1, 1948"
Tabula Poetica: "Eve Clears Her Garden," "Postcard Madonna"
Reach of Song: "Day Trips" (Georgia State Poetry Society, Second Place Prize, formal verse)
Reach of Song: "Gift After Crossing the Threshold" (Georgia State Poetry Society, First Prize, Educator's Award)
Southern Women's Review: "Buddhist Proverb"
Heron Tree: "Swimming Stockbridge Bowl"
Devilfish: "After Dark Llorona"
Calyx: "Rio Grande Llorona," "Clermont Lounge Llorona"

Cover painting by Dylan Swint; author photo by Colin Potts; cover and interior book design by Diane Kistner; Chaparral Pro text and titling

I would like to express gratitude to these teachers, poets, mentors, and friends who helped and encouraged me in the writing of this book: Beth Gylys, David Bottoms, Leon Stokesbury, Kristin Robertson and, of course, the workshop. Thanks to Diane Kistner for all the advice I received during the process of arranging the poems. —CS

About FutureCycle Press

FutureCycle Press is dedicated to publishing lasting English-language poetry books, chapbooks, and anthologies in print-on-demand and Kindle ebook formats. Founded in 2007 by long-time independent editor/publishers and partners Diane Kistner and Robert S. King, the press incorporated as a nonprofit in 2012. A number of our editors are distinguished poets and writers in their own right, and we have been actively involved in the small press movement going back to the early seventies.

The FutureCycle Poetry Book Prize and honorarium is awarded annually for the best full-length volume of poetry we publish in a calendar year. Introduced in 2013, our Good Works projects are anthologies devoted to issues of universal significance, with all proceeds donated to a related worthy cause. Our Selected Poems series highlights contemporary poets with a substantial body of work to their credit; with this series we strive to resurrect work that has had limited distribution and is now out of print.

We are dedicated to giving all of the authors we publish the care their work deserves, making our catalog of titles the most diverse and distinguished it can be, and paying forward any earnings to fund more great books.

We've learned a few things about independent publishing over the years. We've also evolved a unique, resilient publishing model that allows us to focus mainly on vetting and preserving for posterity the most books of exceptional quality without becoming overwhelmed with bookkeeping and mailing, fundraising activities, or taxing editorial and production "bubbles." To find out more about what we are doing, come see us at www.futurecycle.org

The FutureCycle Poetry Book Prize

All full-length volumes of poetry published by FutureCycle Press in a given calendar year are considered for the annual FutureCycle Poetry Book Prize. This allows us to consider each submission on its own merits, outside of the context of a contest. Too, the judges see the finished book, which will have benefitted from the beautiful book design and strong editorial gloss we are famous for.

The book ranked the best in judging is announced as the prize-winner in the subsequent year. There is no fixed monetary award; instead, the winning poet receives an honorarium of 20% of the total net royalties from all poetry books and chapbooks the press sold online in the year the winning book was published. The winner is also accorded the honor of being on the panel of judges for the next year's competition; all judges receive copies of all contending books to keep for their personal library.

www.ingramcontent.com/pod-product-compliance
Lightning Source LLC
Chambersburg PA
CBHW070042110426
42741CB00036B/3161